Mosquitos, Snowbirds & Other Florida Pests

Mosquitos, Snowbirds & Other Florida Pests

MICHAEL A. SISTI

OH!
ORSINI
HOUSE

Mosquitos, Snowbirds and Other Florida Pests

Other books by Michael A. Sisti

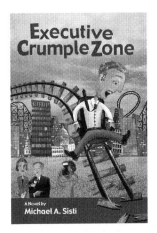

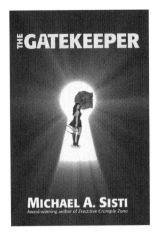

Orsini House, Sarasota, FL 34201
http://MichaelSisti.com

This book is dedicated to my social media family and my neighbors who constantly encourage me to entertain them with my twisted brand of humor.

Acknowledgements

This series of humor books contains a multitude of stories about my friends, neighbors and extended family. Many of you have provided me with countless opportunities to observe stuff that is almost always amusing and many times hilarious. This is a writer's treasure trove of material, so compiling these books was easy, not to mention fun. And in appreciation of the material you unsuspectingly presented, I decided to share the notoriety by using your real names whenever it seemed appropriate. In addition to the stories with a personal connection, there are many anecdotes gleaned from the unique lifestyles of living in New Jersey, Rhode Island and Florida.

In creating the covers for this series, I gave the assignment to Lea Orsini, a young illustrator and graphic designer who has an abundance of talent.

As usual, I had help getting from the rough drafts to finished manuscripts. I enlisted two of my trusted beta readers to review the text and provide input.

My British friend, Alan Nimmey, who now lives Bordeaux read the three books in this series and provided important edits. He was also a great sounding board, as he thoroughly enjoyed the humor.

My second reader was my wife Sara O. Sisti, who despite being familiar with most of the stories, blessed the effort while making her edits. Sara also made suggestions on the graphics for the text and cover.

Foreword
How My Quirky Mind Works

If you read either of my other humor books, you know how I developed the thought process to write stories like these. But if this is your first read of one of my fun-filled compilations, keep reading and learn how the twisted prism of my mind functions.

As far back as I can remember I have always tried to find a way to make the most boring, difficult, and painful tasks fun. This philosophy not only kept me sane and reasonably stress-free, but it also increased my enjoyment of life and gave me a strong appreciation of humor in our lives.

As I refined this process, I developed a keen sense of my surroundings and all the people I encountered. Watching their interactions and delving in their mindset opened a window that constantly feeds my imagination. I can take ordinary events and look at options and scenarios that make them even funnier than they already are.

When I was a school age kid, I enjoyed telling jokes. It was fun to make people laugh. But then I started to tell stories about my family and about incidents that happened with my friends. And those anecdotes were even funnier than the jokes because they were real occurrences with real people.

During that stage of my life, I also discovered my penchant for creativity. As I combined my budding creative thinking with my observational skills, I began to ask 'what if?' whenever I observed a humorous event. And that launched my writing career. I started adding humor to my classroom essays, papers, and letters, and then I began to write short stories. When I got into public speaking, my speeches and talks were sprinkled with my everyday experiences. And when email was introduced to the masses, I had a terrific new outlet to share my goofball ideas and thoughts. I found that the humor also kept people a little off balance. 'Did he really say that?' What did he actually want us to know with that story?'

In the late nineties, while we were living in Rhode Island, I was offered an opportunity to write an online column for a site that offered all kinds of information about Rhode Island. I called my column *Local Color* and my submissions were all about the unusual quirks of Rhode Island and its residents. Those columns provided the basis for another of my humor books and it is named after one of the columns, *The Real Poop on the Dog Track*.

I have now written three novels, and they contain lots of emotion including anger and angst, but I soften the drama with humor, making for entertaining reading.

I hope you have as much fun reading my books as I had writing them (and living them).

Michael A. Sisti

Real Estate: Thinking Outside the Bubble

If you thought that investing in the real estate market is just about the most exciting thing going, I'm about to burst your bubble. Sure, all your friends came back from wintering in Florida, and told you that they became players in the red-hot Florida real estate market. 'You can't miss' they told you. 'Baby boomers by the boatload are buying everything in sight. The prices go up every day. We're making a fortune!'

So let me tell you what's really going on in Florida. It's true, prices are climbing at dramatic, albeit unsustainable rates (35% last year) and nothing stays on the market more than a few days. However, the cost of investing in Florida is very high. Closing costs can run up to $10,000, real estate commissions are 6% to 7%. Then there's insurance - homeowner's, flood, wind and hurricane coverage are all off the charts. Plus, there are HOA application fees, community dues, CDD fees and more that suck even more profit out of your investment. And furthermore if you are going the landlord route, there is no rental market at the rent rates needed to cover these jumbo mortgages and taxes.

Tourists and part-time residents suddenly became 'savvy real estate investors' and bought up all the 'dogs' on the market, and after carrying the soft costs for a year, they hope for a big score next year. Well, guess what? A lot of these people are going to lose their beach wraps because price resistance is starting to creep in. There is not going to be much of a market for that 'cozy, 650 sq. ft. beach cottage in need of a little TLC'. People don't really want a beach cottage that's ten miles from the beach; where the driveway (unpaved) is under water six months of the year; and the living room becomes the master bedroom suite when you pull down the Murphy bed.

Finding a good investment is no easy task. We spent six months rejecting nearly 100 properties ('knowledgeable investors' scooped up everything we turned down). Here's one example. Our realtor arrived at a house a few minutes before our scheduled appointment and rang the doorbell, which was promptly answered by the homeowner. He was wearing a grease-stained tee shirt and neither his hair nor his beard had been cut, washed or groomed in six months. From the open door she could hear the blaring TV and the vicious barking of the pit bull, noise that also carried out the foul smell emanating from the interior. The 'Wild Man from Borneo' invited her in to preview the house, but she wisely chose to wait for us outside in the heat.

We arrived and went into the living room, which was cluttered with dilapidated furniture, used bath fixtures and other construction debris. Sara pointed to the blaring cartoons on TV and shouted, 'You have kids?' He responded, 'No, I live here alone.' The entire house looked like the aftermath of a hurricane, except the garage, which housed a sleek 911 Porsche. The home's asking price was $389,000 and I told my realtor that I would consider it at $250,000, only if he threw in the car.

At another location, a rental apartment complex was going condo as people waited in line overnight in order to purchase one of these 35 year-old, must-have units, which were being sold 'sight unseen, as-is'. It was reminiscent of buying rock concert tickets . . . without knowing who was playing.

So here's my advice for all you wannabe real estate tycoons. 'Buy high, sell low, but do a lot of deals so you can make up the shortfall on volume.'

6

They're Not Anchors, They're Slugs

So here comes hurricane number four to further shatter what started out to be a relaxing, tranquil year. Hurricane Jeanne was supposed to be the mildest of them all, so none of us really prepared for the storm. We didn't even buy extra toilet paper. We've been hearing about this storm for weeks to the point where we are all numb.

Have you ever noticed that in reporting every pending natural disaster, the meteorologists are like teenagers before their first date? And the anticipation is always far more exciting, titillating, and spectacular than the actual event.

Sunday morning, I got up at six, just as the wind and rain began. I made a mug of tea, got into my reclining lounge chair, fastened my seatbelt and turned on the TV. I had a choice of Weather Central, Storm Team Now, Eye on the Sky, or Hurricane Havoc (my personal favorite). Being an equal opportunity viewer, I decided to give them all a shot (except NBC - I had already emailed them that I would never watch their politically biased, fake news network again). So here I am, channel surfing the news and weather stations to find out just how bad we are going to be hit. Instead of telling me whether I should evacuate or book a tee time, they show me a guy standing on a beach on the East Coast.

'This is Mosely Vacuous at Storm Tracker Headquarters bringing you the latest information to protect your life and those of your loved ones. As you know we're facing the threat of another killer hurricane, and it could get you no matter where you're hiding.

We're going to go to correspondent Joe Schmacone, who is at the beach on Hutchinson Island where they just evacuated everyone living in tents and lean-tos. But first we'll take a commercial break and bring you a message from Prison Specialties, makers of hurricane shutters and other confining products. Don't move that dial.'

'Joe, can you hear us?' (Pause) 'Hi. This is Joe Schmacone from W-A-C-K, a Clearhead Communications station in Stuart Florida. (Did you ever notice that in every natural disaster, there is always some dumb reporter out in the middle of it getting his wet ass pounded?) I am standing on the beach at Hutchinson Island, in the exact spot where in 1905 Hurricane Godzilla came ashore. That hurricane, as you may remember, caused a storm surge of 20 feet. If that were to happen today, the water level would be fourteen feet above my head.' (Duh.)

'And you can't believe the strength of the wind. I can hardly stand up.' (At this point, the producer whispers to Joe, through his ear-piece, 'Joe, you're leaning the wrong way. The wind is coming from the south. No. That's from your left.')

Adjusting his stance, Joe continues, 'The exact location of the eye of this fierce hurricane is 40.5 degrees north and 73.6 degrees east.' (How am I supposed to figure out where the storm is from that information? But there's more.) 'This is a strong Category One hurricane (the weakest category) with sustained winds of 26 miles per hour and gusts to 34.9 miles per hour, but they could go as high 75 or 76 miles per hour. So get to your safe rooms right away! We're getting reports that there may be a Level Two, flatulating micro-burst event, which will trigger a defecating wind shear and possible sporadic tornadic activity. The storm is registering 972 millibars (that's weatherspeak for Milky Way Bars, the number of which you would have to eat to create the energy of the storm for one nanosecond.) The storm is tracking north-northeast at 12 miles per hour and will dump two to four inches of rain per hour. This is gonna be one mother of a hurricane! Wow, that fuckin' flying tree branch just missed my head. This is Joe Schmacone, WAKO TV, signing off. Back to you, Mose.'

At that point, I went out to the garage to find a suitable golf club to throw through the TV screen. But when I returned to the den with my oversized Seismic Slammer Driver, the power had gone off, mercifully relieving me of having to watch any more TV weather anchors for the remainder of the day. And I can relax in the fact that in a couple of months, these same storms will all be tracking north along the Atlantic to give New Englanders the blizzard conditions from those famous Nor'easters.

Snowbird Sightings

It's winter in the northern hemisphere with the temperatures plunging and the snow flying. That's the signal for the Snowbirds to start migrating to Florida. It begins in late December and continues until the end of April, when they all find their way back to their home state, or their province in Canada. It starts at 4:30 A.M. on December 26th, with everyone driving down Route 95 or Route 75 to Florida. It seemed like every big Caddy and Lincoln was on the road that morning.

This time of year there's this game that's played in Florida at all the resort communities. It's spotting Snowbirds and it's really easy. You see in the winter, the Florida residents wear winter clothes, turtlenecks and sweaters; and they wear appropriate colors, navies, browns and grays. They just wear lighter weight versions of what is sold in the northeast. The daytime temperature in southwest Florida ranges from the fifties to the eighties. The Snowbirds on the other hand have left all their winter clothes at home and packed only their beachwear.

There are usually a few days when a cold spell hits Florida and the temperature plunges to 40 in the morning, and sometime it reaches 32. On the golf course on those mornings, you can always spot the Canadians. While us locals are wearing long pants, jackets, and ear muffs, the Canucks are in their shorts and collared tee shirts.

The other day we were in a supermarket, doing some grocery shopping when I spot a Snowbird in aisle six. She was wearing a two-piece, large floral print ensemble in magenta, orange, yellow and lime with a headscarf in the same colors. Her acrylic-sole wedgies had matching silk flowers on the straps, as did her necklace and earring's. This was an outfit that gives cruise wear a bad name. And her tan was two shades this side of cappuccino. Without indicating whom I was referring to, I said to Sara, "Do you think she's from around here?" Giggle, Giggle.

Since Sarasota has some of the most beautiful beaches in the world, we often get our exercise by walking a couple of miles along the beach in the early morning. Last week we passed a middle-aged man sitting in a lounge chair on Siesta Beach. Although his sun-induced milk chocolate coloring ran from his bald head to the balls of his feet, he was out there reinforcing his tan. In addition, he had a cigar in one hand, a super-size bag of French fries in his lap and a shaker of pina coladas sitting on his cooler. It was nine-thirty in the morning. We took bets guessing what time the Snowbird ambulance would come for him. We Floridians, contrary to popular belief, never expose our bodies to harmful sunrays, so our skin is always a natural color. And despite all the sun block and avoidance of excessive sun, we still get keratosis, basal cells, melanoma, etc.

Later that day we were on line at the farm market. The woman in front of us was wearing hot pink, Spandex Capri's, just one size too small for her generous figure. Across the pants seat was screened the name of our beautiful city. The type had originally been set in Helvetica Bold Condensed, but now it was Helvetica Extra Bold Extra Wide. I was amazed that she would want to bring even more attention to her ample back porch (more like pavilion), but Sara found something positive in this bold statement. She turned to me and whispered, 'Look at that. She named her left cheek after me.'

Pissed Off!

My good friend Larry is in town for his customary mid-summer business trip. After a couple of lonely nights without his main squeeze Jo, Larry decided to stop by a local club for a few drinks. As he entered the boisterous, chemically induced energy of GRUNGE, lights started flashing, sirens went off, and a spotlight brought everyone's attention to Larry. And everyone began cheering. It seems that he was the club's 10,000th visitor this year, entitling him to a free lap dance by the Biggest Loser runner-up, Thighs Thigpen. The caveat, however, was that the dance was going to be performed on a bicycle seat.

When the weight of all this spandex-encased Jello was compressed onto that one-inch wide portion of the seat, it caused Larry to experience a testicular trauma, resulting in a ruptured blood vessel in his prostate. So, what started out as a few drinks in Cougar-Town ends up being an admission to Sarasota Hospital's ER.

The doctor, eager to determine the extent of the damage, decided on a camera probe to get up close and personal, so to speak. I can understand employing a high definition camera, but the zoom lens was overkill. Once Dr. Death diagnosed the extent of the damage, he ordered an irrigation procedure to stop the bleeding and cleanse the organs. This treatment was achieved by the rectal insertion of a 10" Rainbird oscillating spray nozzle attached to a backflow valve. Being a *Green* facility, Sarasota Hospital uses only reclaimed water for these procedures. And as soon as his urine is clear he will be released.

As of today, Larry is lying in a puddle of pond scum, with water leaking out of every orifice in his body, but his stream is still the color of lipstick. If it doesn't clear up soon, he may have to switch to a drip irrigation system. That gets installed in another place.

Pray for Larry as he pisses away his days in Sarasota.

Brown Alert

I was driving down I75, approaching University Parkway, when the overhead message board started flashing – Brown Alert! A French Bulldog had gone missing in the vicinity of University Parkway. If you're not familiar with the breed, they are a cross between a bulldog and Chihuahua, with some added DNA from Charles De Gaulle. They are so ugly that they are actually cute. And they smile like humans, which is really freaky.

After seeing the message, I immediately called the Brown Alert Hotline and spoke to the K911 Operator. She told me a dog sitter that had called in was frantic and almost incoherent. The dog, who answered to Souffle or Shithead or something unintelligible apparently got out through an open back door and ran away.

I raced home and sure enough, there was my neighbor, holding her dog on a leash plus an empty leash, standing in the street frantic with terror. The missing dog belonged to her daughter, who recently became a TV personality, providing interviews of sports celebrities. And my neighbor was caring for her daughter's dog. She told me her husband Bobby left the back door open and the dog got out and disappeared. Of course, it's always Bobby's fault, the guy who doesn't have any faults. They had been driving around the neighborhood for two hours in their golf cart, as well as combing the common area woods, but no Souffle. There wasn't even a stray poop on the street to indicate that the dog had been in the area. So it was a case of an obvious dognapping. And now that it was known that its owner was a national TV celebrity, she was probably being contacted for a ransom payment.

As the Community Chairman, I feel a strong responsibility for my neighbors. Despite most of them having retired as titans of industry, they have become very dependent on me. So I went home very upset. I didn't eat dinner and had a fitful night's sleep. The next morning, Sara drove out early to get to the Dillard's Sale by the time that their doors opened at 7. And she saw Bobby in front of his house, smiling broadly, kind of like a French bulldog. (It's true. After a while, you start to look like your pet.) Well, it turns out the dog was safely returned. Souffle, on making his escape, had raced up the street to another neighbor's house to play with her two pet squirrels (they may be dogs but they're the size of squirrels). While there, after not being fed for days, Souffle devoured both the other two dog's food. Recognizing Souffle, the neighbor immediately brought him home before he ate her dinner and all the food in the pantry.

I still haven't recovered from the event. So now I drive up and down I75, watching the message board for a Silver Alert when one of my neighbor's husbands inevitably disappears.

Mosquitos, Snowbirds and Other Florida Pests

I've put together some handy information that you will need when you move to Florida.

Traffic lights can take up to seven minutes to turn green, so seniors use the time to take naps. And they don't appreciate it when you blast your horn if they don't move quickly enough when the light changes.

The most popular restaurants are the all-you-can-eat lunch buffets. Women arrive with handbags the size of knapsacks, and fill them with rolls, butter, vegetables and entrees. And that becomes their dinner that night. Once a week, seniors go out for the early-bird dinners. They get there at five and leave by six. The restaurants close by eight, and the street lights go off at nine.

The men play golf three times a week, and the women play cards and mahjong. But next to bingo, gossiping is the most popular pastime.

You also need to understand about dress codes. The fashion police are everywhere. Snowbirds are required to wear resort apparel all the time. This includes beach attire all day long, but more formalwear in the evening. For the men, plaid pants and colorful, floral-print shirts, with white patent leather shoes and belts are still in style. Women have more latitude, as long as they are overdressed in last year's summer fashion styles. Canadian men and Minnesotans wear shorts and collared tee shirts, regardless how far below freezing the temperature falls. By contrast, year-round residents wear seasonally-appropriate trends and colors.

Despite popular belief, the state is not overrun with bugs. In most areas mosquitos are controlled with selective spraying, and stocking ponds and lakes with larvae-eating fish. Although the palmetto bug (oversize cockroach) is the state pet, they are not nearly as plentiful as roaches in New York City.

There are lots of alligators in Florida. I mean a shitload in many areas, especially golf courses. But they are docile animals for the most part. But don't get down to their level. When you stand near them, you are four or five feet higher than them, and that makes them afraid of you. If you get down on your hands and knees and reach into a lake to retrieve you golf ball, well you no longer look intimidating to them. So you just lost your balls, and your right arm. Also, don't sit on a footbridge and dangle your feet. Alligators like toes.

Minding the Neighborhood

October 1

Hi Neighbors,

By way of introduction, for those of you who don't know me, I am Michael Sisti, and I am the new Committee Chairman for Lennox Gardens.

I'm looking forward to this challenge as it gives me an opportunity to be of service to my neighbors. My goal as chairman is to improve the social interaction among the LG residents, as well as with all the new homeowners from the Lansdowne neighborhood adjacent to ours. Since they share our pool and workout facility, we want to include them in as many activities as possible.

My responsibilities, as I understand them are to attend Association meetings, make decisions on behalf of the neighborhood, and disseminate information to the LG homeowners. In addition, I will attempt to help anyone needing assistance, information or resources, to the best of my ability. Just so we're clear, please be advised that I have very little patience for whiners and crybabies. And before being volunteered for this position, I have been assured that there are none living in Lennox Gardens. So my job should be easy.

November 18

Since I became the Neighborhood Chairman, people have been reaching out to me to organize certain events, or resolve community issues and problems that are either real or imagined. And while I would like to satisfy all these requests, my time is limited. I am ungainfully employed as an author, lecturer and consultant, for all that entails. And recognizing that most of the people that are making these requests are retired and looking for exciting new challenges, I usually ask them to take the lead on their suggested activity. And I've noticed, that is the point when they disappear. So now, every time I drive on I75 and see the Silver Alert Advisories, it makes me wonder if those are my missing neighbors.

December 10

The Pool heater broke down again. The temporary solution is to use the back-up unit, which is not as effective as the main heater. In the meantime, the pool water is not at the temperature it should be. But it is warmer than the water in New York Harbor, and certainly cleaner.

I even thought about making the repairs myself, but the monkey stole my wrench.

January 10

In answer to some of your questions - Yes, Sara and I are going to Thailand for the month of February. And we will not be here to take care of your incessant needs. In fact, while we are gone, there will be no grief counseling if you suffer Separation Anxiety Syndrome. But if you want to ensure that you will be stress-free and happy while we're gone, why don't some of you arrange a cocktail party at the pool in late February, or get the next couples golf outing organized for early March, or help Monroe set up another Men's 9-hole golf game in early February. We really need help with these initiatives. But if none of this appeals to you, then you might try medical marijuana.

March 16

If a couple of you buff hunks could help me unwrap and move the new pool furniture tomorrow or Tuesday morning, we could get it done in a half hour or less. Let me know if you are available either morning. Thanks.

As soon as some women responded with their offer to help, the men came out of the woodwork. (Egos can be so fragile.) So I want to thank all of you ladies who volunteered, and let you know that your services will not be needed. We now have plenty of manly men to handle this manly task. With all this available muscle, the task will be done in about five minutes. We'll move the furniture on Tuesday morning at 9:30. Hardhats not required. Advil will be provided.

April 1
As mentioned in a previous email, next Wednesday, the Ladies Happy Hour will be expanded to a full-blown party that includes the guys. So bring something to eat and something to drink, and plan on staying for the full evening. The men are playing golf earlier, and will join the fun immediately following the F-bomb competition on the course. Unfortunately, they will be all cranky, sweaty and smelly, but isn't that how they usually show up for a party?

So with everyone invited, let's have a full-attendance event before the Snowbirds anxiously head back north. They hear the ice is just starting to come out of the lakes, and the black flies will fill the woods in a few weeks.

August 30
I have been getting lots of frantic emails and phone calls from all of you who are out of town. Yes, there is a major, Category Five hurricane coming and it will hit Florida. Why are you asking me if it will hit Sarasota? I'm not a meteorologist. Aren't you watching the news?

I'm certain that before you left for your homes up north, you completed your due diligence and took all the recommended steps to protect your property from storm damage. All the houses in our community are built to hurricane code, so they should easily survive without any major damage. See you when you get back in the late fall.

September 8

This is very troubling. In the last 24 hours, I've received dozens of emails, phone calls, and text messages, some in the middle of the night, all wanting me to go to your houses and secure patio furniture, flower pots and other personal property that were not properly stored away before heading north. What were you thinking? How could you leave in the spring and not store away your outdoor furniture and accessories? Well, you're on your own.

I'm getting ready to hunker down and ride out this monster storm, so there is no way I can take care of your houses at the same time.

September 13

The storm is over and the power just came back on. Most of the heaviest winds and rain missed us completely when the eye shifted to the east. But we did get 90-mile an hour wind gusts.

I can see many tree limbs down around the neighborhood, and lots of debris, but I didn't go house to house to check damage. And yes there is patio furniture strewn around the neighborhood, and broken flower pots in the street, pools and lakes. I can't tell who any of it belongs to. You'll have to do that when you return.

I am sorry that I couldn't take care of your houses and stuff before the storm, but I'm really surprised and disappointed in many of the negative comments I received.

September 14

I really don't appreciate the nasty emails and threatening phone messages I'm getting. It wasn't my job to secure your outdoor furniture and accessories.

And no, I didn't get my trees trimmed free back in the spring because I'm the chairman. I paid just like the rest of you.

I especially take offense to the bitch that made the disparaging comments about the color of my house. It is not the only pink house in four states. And if it bothers you that much, take up a collection and have it painted a different color. I'm thinking of orange with lavender trim.

I'm the Neighborhood Chair, not your goddamn caretaker. If you don't like the job I'm doing, then you can take it and shove it up your ass.

So to all of you, "Go fuck off!"

The Exodus

"And the Chosen People will go out and wander into the desert for 40 years."

Drawing on his roots and culture found in the deep recesses of the Bible, Beloved Peter has chosen to take his beloved spouse and go out and live in the wilderness, not far from the son he begat, who now resides in the modern city of Sodom & Gomorrah (Hollywood). And Peter, bound by his chosen vocation, will spend these 40 years wandering in the desert (Palm Springs) in search of his lost ball while avoiding the serpents.

You are invited to reflect upon the countless reasons to celebrate the departure of our loved one, as may please your mind. Be it the pieces of silver you wagered and lost during your golf games over the years, or his amazing recall of ancient golf rules from the Old Testament that always favored his position, now is the time to forgive and rejoice. And it is also time to realize that there will be no recourse of ever regaining the hoard of silver that will now travel onto the desert with Beloved Peter.

Those of you who wish to celebrate Peter's parting of The Misty Creek, and his journey with his devoted spouse, Rachel of Nazareth, are invited to witness the Last Supper and drinketh from the chalice, the wine from the water urn that Peter hath blessed and miraculously turned into vintage Mogen David Concord. (The cheap bastard didn't want to spend money on good wine.)

The Last Supper, which usually precedes a crucifixion, will be held in the halls of Misty Creek on Friday, March 18. And since there will be room at the table for a limited number of disciples and their brethren, go forth and partake at your own table with your fellow tribesmen, where there will be less chance of a betrayer in your midst, and make a toast with your blessed wine. (Hopefully, a better brand.)

Call Mary Magdalene, or one of her handmaidens at The Misty Creek and make your own reservation to witness and cheer on The Exodus. And don't hesitate to invite other believers and nonbelievers who wish to witness these miracles, and consume some of the fishes and loaves.

A Reading from the Book of Michael, The beloved older scribe of the Very Old Testament

Getting Wired

After we announced with much fanfare that we had cancelled our landline as a result of the never-ending nightmare with Comcast, something changed. After weeks of blissful silence, the phone suddenly rang yesterday. Since I was busy doing laundry, vacuuming, and ironing Sara's socks, she answered the phone expecting a dead line. But it was a Comcast representative calling to tell us that they were able to get our old phone number transferred to our new home. So we now have our landline back.

That's the good news. So here's the black cloud that is connected to the silver lining. A couple of days ago Sara and I both lost our email accounts with no warning or explanation. I again started a telethon with Comcast and got nowhere. Sara went to the University Park community office where they negotiate the Comcast contract for all residents, and spoke to the president of the Community Association to explain our plight. She said that she would intervene on our behalf. She called back later and assured me that Comcast was on the case. She gave me the regular Comcast phone number (1-800-TRAGEDY) and told me to ask for the Center of Excellence, a special department that was expecting my call. When I stopped laughing at the name I called. And that's when the fun began.

First the mechanical operator asked me to key in the phone number connected with the account. Since we had cancelled the new number they gave us when we moved, there was no such number, so I dialed 0. And the voice said, 'I don't recognize that number.' I then keyed the only other number that could get her attention, 9-1-1. 'I don't recognize that number. Good-bye.' I called back and listened for a prompt for people that don't have an account, but want to become a Comcast customer. Of course, I can't imagine that any of those people are left on this planet. I immediately got a breathless sales rep anxious to sell me the Triple Play Ultimate Bundle with 24/7 Total Sports Package including Fantasy Football stats, 2,000 video games a week, and 27 channels of X-rated programming. I explained that I was already a customer, albeit a disgruntled one, and wanted to be transferred to the Center of Excellence. As expected, he never heard of that department, so he handed the call off to the Disenchanted Customer Recovery Department. After one hour, and five transfers later I finally got someone with an IQ that registered above 67. Her name was Maxie Braynefott. And she was in the Raging Homicidal Customer Hotline. She couldn't explain why we don't have email, but she said that she could fix it within 24 hours. And she would call back, something that has happened only once in six weeks. And without her callback, providing us with new passwords, we would never be able access our email. That was three days ago, and we're still staring at the phone.

So today, when the Comcast rep called about our phone service, I asked him about the email and he got it restored in five minutes. However, they lost all our email over the past several days. So if you sent us something important like putting us in your will, please resend it.

Postscript. Comcast has had to change the name of the Center of Excellence. There is no word in the English language to describe their service that is so diabolically awful it causes anxiety attacks. Since they couldn't come up with an appropriate name to replace Excellence, they had to make one up. It's called Xfinity. So if you're experiencing problems like mine, Call Comcast and ask for the Center of Xfinity.

Shock Therapy

If you were planning to take a swim in the community pool during this afternoon's electrical storm, I would advise you to postpone it. The pool is receiving a shock treatment for algae spots (they're like age spots on your hands). It will reopen tomorrow.

You can imagine my shock when I went there yesterday morning to find the pool wrapped in crime scene tape. I even looked for blood spatter, just like on TV.

And speaking of electric, I was further shocked when I entered the exercise facility to find the AC on 72 and the TV blaring at nobody. When you finish your workout, please turn off the TV and raise the AC to 79. We're looking for ways to reduce our costs, and this is a factor. The forensic investigation determined that the perpetrator was an absent-minded, conservative, fake-news junkie. The TV setting was on Fox News.

Sara and I went to work out yesterday to put in some pain with the hope of a small gain. When I left, my waist was still the same size, but my smile was twice as large. (not sure what that weighs) The Comcast technician was also there. To complete the installation of the cable service. But rather than installing the basic box, we got the premium box with all the channels, voice control, etc. just like you have at home. He installed the Full Monty. Speaking of which, you can even watch that On Demand. But wait, there's more. We have some special programming for your workout entertainment. Included in the line-up is Real Housewives of Jakarta, Afraid and Naked in Botswana, America's Got Freeloaders, Walmart Fashionistas, and Who Wants To Be A Brazilionaire?

But don't expect to download your favorite pay-per-view movies. They're blocked. There is wi-fi that can be accessed as far away as the parking lot. You can now lounge around and call your family in the Seychelles or the Maldives, or wherever they live, from the comfort of the deck chairs.

So now you have no excuse for not getting that flabby body in shape. You can distract yourselves from the pain of exercise by watching TV on our new flat screen. And as requested by some of you, I changed the treadmill to miles from kilometers. So you have to walk that much further to hit your numbers.

The other good news is that the Universal Bench is repaired, so Pump, Baby, Pump.

I've been getting emails from several of you thanking me for the effort at the pool and the fitness center. But please understand that I did not do the repairs or installations myself. I contacted Todd from the property manager's office, and he brought in the service vendors to make all the upgrades and repairs.

Matt (Lansdowne Chair) spearheaded the furniture purchase, also working with Todd. I had very little involvement in that project.

And also recognize that I do not have everything under control. Just ask Sara.

With that said, I do appreciate your positive comments. Of course, a bottle of wine would also be a nice gesture.

Unlisted Number

Important Announcement

In response to your many frantic calls, I was able to determine the cause of the pool being closed today. Although I must say that I'm taken aback that so many of you are calling about the pool on the coldest day we've had in the last seven months. The temperature will not reach 50 today, and that is the highest we can expect for the rest of the week. Nighttime temperatures will plunge into the mid-thirties. So what's all the urgency to take a swim in our outdoor pool?

After several phone calls to Comcast and the staff at the property management office, I learned that the Manatee Health Department made an unscheduled inspection yesterday and closed the pool because the emergency phone wasn't working. What's really interesting is that the lock on the childproof entry gate was damaged in last week's storm, and doesn't lock the gate. That serious violation was overlooked by the inspector, while the phone thing raised havoc.

Those of you that called the pool to reserve your favorite lounge chair and extra towels probably got a busy signal.

The out-of-service phone is a violation of Rule #38291960490-B, Section 8 of the Practical Solutions Handbook of the Manatee County Health Code. The ordinance does not take into consideration that everyone has a cell phone these days, and that we have wi-fi at the pool. The culprit, and you probably won't believe this, happens to be Comcast. They turned off the phone when the new contract went into effect, because the former property manager neglected to factor into the contract the handful of emergency phones throughout the campus that were provided at no charge. So we are now paying $65 per phone per month, because they are not "residential" phones. Their VP of Brand Image at Comcast should get a raise for that decision.

The new phone service that was installed this morning only allows calls outbound calls to 911. So for those of you that have been using the pool phone to call your relatives Kazakhstan will have to find an alternate way to communicate with them.

But back to reality. The pool is open just in time for your cool-down swim this afternoon. Also, the weekly Synchronized Swimming classes and the High Diving Competition will resume later this week. Call the pool for starting times and reservations.

I Love Comcast

Just when you thought it was safe to start using your email account again, I get back into town. So, yes, you have to block me again, if you are tired of my rants.

I returned late last night to two cubic feet of mail, and buried in the pile was a slick brochure from everyone's favorite TV and Internet service - Comcast. The mailer I got is in full color and personalized with my name and address inside and the phone number (1-800-XFINITY) to call for my appointment for the fiber optic installation. Yes, that's the same number that you received last week. If you got to call that number, you probably found out that nobody at that location can schedule your service. I spent a couple of hours and three phone calls (still awaiting their fourth return call) trying to schedule my install, only to find out who I should actually be calling for the service. And as the neighborhood chair, I also want to find out how they are going to handle 1,200 requests from University Park residents who were sent the wrong phone number for installation.

If you can't get to the right department to schedule your installation, call 1-800-COMCAST. That's actually the department that is able handle your request. I fortunately had that number from a previous Comcast nightmare, and when I called it, I immediately got the appointment set up without any hassle. Of course, they never showed up.

The Cheap Seats

When we decided to fly to New Jersey for a family wedding, Sara got online to book our flights. We usually fly Southwest, as they offer the best fares of the large carriers. And they advertise them as *Tranfarency*. Well, they'll need to change that to *Transfantasy*. Their rates are right up there with the high price leaders despite their bare bones service. So I told Sara to try the smaller discount airlines.

And sure enough, she found flights from nearby Myakka Crop-dusting Co-op Field to Alamuchy, NJ for only $79 on Egregious Airlines, which she quickly booked. Alamuchy is a remote wilderness area in the New Jersey hills. The terminal is a Quonset hut with no electronics of any kind. The TSA screening is handled by a former women's prison warden, who hand searches every passenger.

Three days after booking, we got an email from the carrier saying, 'Thank you for becoming an Egregious Flyer. We received payment for your flight, but you didn't select your seats. Please read and agree to the terms in the pull-down menu, and then select and pay for your seats. Our standard seat with non-reclining back is $48. There are four of those middle-row seats still available. For an extra $60, you can upgrade to our deluxe reclining seats, which offer extra leg and headroom, plus early boarding and preferred overhead bin selection. For our wide-body passengers, we offer additional options for those upgraded passengers. If your waist is larger than 48", you can order a seatbelt extender in various sizes, starting at 12" at $2 per inch, which includes your weight surcharge.'

Reading the terms further I learned that each passenger is entitled to one carry-on plus a purse. For men, wallets are considered a carry-on. The maximum dimensions for the carry-on are equivalent to the size of a large handbag, so just about everything must be checked at $50 per bag. If you check in at the counter, there's a $5 convenience fee, and at the curb it's only $2, plus the requisite tip to ensure your luggage gets to the right destination.

The flight was pleasant, but uneventful. They offered water at $1.50, but ice was extra, and there was no food service. Landing on a gravel runway was a new experience, but it turned out to be a little softer, albeit with some sliding and fishtailing. The 'Welcome to the Garden State' sign sharply contradicted the gray skies, bare trees, brown grass, plus the 22-degree temperature and winds gusting to 40 mph. Now that's *Transfarency*.

Lake Tahoe Adventure

On Saturday, Jan. 25th, we left frosty Sarasota (early morning temps around 30) for a ski vacation in sunny Lake Tahoe with our longtime friends Hugo and Lucille. Florida is experiencing record lows and the temperatures in Tahoe were averaging 25 degrees higher than normal. It seemed strange to go skiing where the temperature was warmer than Sarasota. The lake is on the California/Nevada border, in the Sierra Nevada Mountains. It's one of the deepest lakes in the world and contains more water than any of the Great Lakes. And the surrounding mountains rise to more than 10,000 ft.

We flew into Reno, which has the nearest major airport to the ski resorts. When gambling became legal in Nevada, Reno was known as 'The Biggest Little City in America.' Now, in Las Vegas, which has become the gambling Mecca, Reno is referred to as 'The World's Largest Trailer Park.'

The ride from Reno is a little over an hour, and you drive out of the desert and through the mountain pass to the ski areas. Our condo, built into the side of the mountain at 7,500 ft., faced the parched desert, even though we were surrounded by snow. When you ski Heavenly, you can stand at the top of the mountain and see the lake on one side, in the center of all the snow-covered mountains, and the brown desert on the other side. It's an amazing contrast.

The first night there we went to the casino and made a small deposit. We then went to the buffet restaurant at the top of the hotel/casino, where you can have all of the steam-tray food you can eat for $19. When they seated us, we looked around and realized that we were in the midst of more overweight people than we have ever seen in our lives. These weren't just large people, they were gargantuan, and they were inhaling food like industrial vacuum cleaners. It was like being at a co-ed Sumo Wrestling Convention. And it was an insurance actuary's worst nightmare! Even the chairs were extra large to accommodate the super-sized butts. I noticed that there was no music playing in the dining room. I assumed that the management feared that if everyone started dancing, the restaurant might fall through to the casino, 12 floors below.

On the morning of our fourth day, we rode three lifts to the top of Heavenly. There we took some pictures and started skiing down a wide-open intermediate run. At a point where it intersected another trail, we yelled to Sara, who was leading the group, to turn right. Unfortunately, she was just starting a left turn, and as she tried to abruptly change direction, she fell, releasing both skis. Although it looked innocuous, the fall was hard enough to break her left leg just below the knee. She was taken off the mountain in a sled, a terrifying experience in itself. I then eased her into our rental car and I rushed her to the hospital emergency room ten miles away, an even more terrifying experience.

She required surgery to insert five pins and a plate, plus a bone graft. The surgery, however, was a piece of cake compared with getting her back to the condo. That required negotiating down three flights of stairs to get into the unit. She couldn't use a walker on the narrow, icy stairs. My suggestion was to lay her on a snowboard and have Hugo catch her at the bottom of each landing. Sara rejected this idea, so we put her in a plastic patio chair and carried her down.

The last hurdle was getting to the airport. We had a mid-size Buick for five people (Lucille's son Michael joined us during the week) and lots of luggage, including Michael's snowboard. We stuffed the trunk with the suitcases, lashed the snowboard bag to the roof rack and tried to squeeze the five people and four boot bags into the less-than-full-size car. Again, I came up with a creative solution. We could tie Sara to the roof rack with the snowboard (she could even lie down). This way her leg could remain in an extended position in the full leg cast. She told me what I could do with the roof rack and even tried to put her foot, cast and all, in a place where it wouldn't fit. We managed to get us all in, with one boot bag propping up Sara's leg and another bag in Hugo's lap.

In order to make it home, we overcame a phone call (never documented) to confirm reservations and advise the airline of Sara's situation; an oversold flight that mysteriously lost our seat confirmation; a piece of luggage that tested positive for nitroglycerine (I thought that was going to result in a cavity search); and two no-show wheelchair assistants. And we made it door-to-door in only 11 fun-filled hours on two bags of peanuts and two glasses of water.

Next year we're going to try something safer, like hang-gliding.

Men at Play

Recently, I played in a foursome at Misty Creek and had the opportunity to spend lots of time observing the group in front of us as they tried their skills against this difficult course. Each golfer in this group drove his own cart. The reason, we learned was to speed up play. The outcome was questionable.

On the first hole, three of the golfers were at the green, while the fourth (We'll call him Player A) was still in the fairway, playing his approach shot. At a distance of about 120 yards, he got out of his cart, walked the five feet to the ball, checked the lie and returned to the cart. He then rummaged around the bag, selecting three clubs, and stepped to the ball. Choosing one of the clubs, and dropping the other two onto the grass, he took three practice swings, each stopping at the ground. He then set up and took a different swing as he hit the ball. While we couldn't follow the ball flight from our position on the tee, we did notice that he drove the cart about 50 yards forward and way into the right rough near the tree line, and repeated the procedure.

On the second hole, we arrived at the tee, just as they were completing their drives. We then watched this Keystone Kops routine as they scattered all over the fairway, surrounding glades and bushes in search of their balls. At the completion of the hole, the four golfers walked off the green to their carts. When Player A got to the cart path, he realized that his cart was parked in the No Cart Area on the opposite side of the green. As he turned and went the other way, he realized that he also left his wedge on the green.

On the next hole, as we stood in the fairway and watched the foursome complete their putts and walk off, Player C began to give the other golfers the play-

play of the entire, previous night's Yankee game. Although we couldn't hear what he was saying, from the body language we were convinced that the Yanks lost.

As the round progressed, it became obvious that this group of golfers (and I use the word loosely) was having the time of their lives, and the round of their careers. They were constantly shouting cheers and yelling boisterously, giving high fives, butt bumps, and all. We felt that this was much better than listening to F-bombs all day long, even though it was very distracting.

The ninth hole presented us with a fascinating sight that just has to be shared. Standing on the tee box, we watched the fearless foursome take their second shots. Player A stood by his ball, which was less than 10 yards ahead of Player B's ball. Player B was searching the reeds for his ball, retrieved it, dropped it and took his next shot. During this time, instead of helping B, we were mesmerized as Mr. A took eleven practice strokes. He then stepped up to his ball, took three more practice swings, and then chunked his shot. And that's when he noticed Player B behind him. By this time the other two players were already at the green, dodging the incoming shots.

When we were on the tenth fairway, I was in the act of hitting my iron shot, when someone in their group, now on the eleventh tee, started sounding his cart horn. Of course, I completely miss-hit my shot slicing it 30 yards off line. But hey, if they blew their horn, someone must have been in grave danger. So what's a bad shot when a life may have been saved? We learned later, that the horn blast was to the foursome in front of them, because they took too long in search of a lost ball.

The Coup de Grass came on the par three, 17th hole. We waited interminably long for the golfers to get to the green with the flag way in the back, chip on and then putt out. Once the hole was completed, they left the green to go to eighteen - all except the A Player. He had to walk back about thirty yards off the front of the green to where his cart was parked, again in a no-cart zone. As he got in and started to drive off, he suddenly stopped to pick up one of his clubs that was lying in the rough. He then drove another ten yards, and found another of his clubs. As compassionate golfers, rather than getting angry, we felt for this poor soul. He was obviously a new golfer, and his friends hadn't yet explained the concept of preparation, ready golf, and the simple steps that lead to a four-hour round.

Well, finally they finished eighteen, congratulating each other, shaking hands and collecting their clubs before leaving the green and returning to their carts. And as it turned out, using multiple carts did save time. They completed the round in four hours and fifty-five minutes. Had they taken only two carts, who knows? The round could have lasted six hours.

The Wild, Wild West

My image of the wild west was always shoot-em-up cowboys taking out the bad guys. But on our first visit to Tucson, I learned a completely different meaning. The wild west actually consists of fascinating wild life. Within a 48-hour period I saw an adult bobcat, considerably larger than its Florida cousins, a lone coyote, a prairie dog, a Gila monster, several roadrunners, covies of quail, a pack of mule deer, a herd of javalinos, and a shitload of rabbits.

The Gila monster sighting was the most exciting. My host Bruce, who has lived in Tucson for forty years, has only seen three during all that time, and we were within a couple of feet of this beautiful reptile.

Tucson is a stark environment, whose beauty is in its rugged 10,000-foot rock-face mountains, and the desert with its abundant, prickly vegetation that remarkably survives with almost no water. Often referred to as a wasteland, it is anything but. The saguaros cacti are majestic, growing only an inch a year, and not developing arms until they are at least 65 years old. In this part of the southwest, they grow profusely everywhere, usually in the shadow of mesquite trees. It is hard to imagine seeing so many living objects that are hundreds of years old everywhere you look.

While the natural scenery is breathtaking, downtown Tucson is the real wasteland. There are only a handful of modern high-rise buildings, and most city blocks have at least half the land area vacant. There is construction everywhere, but it's all municipal projects, mostly road improvements and a boondoggle trolley line that has been under construction for decades. The population is overwhelmingly Hispanic and it's anyone's guess what percentage are undocumented.

After all, we are only miles from the border. Our hosts, Bruce & Marianne took us to dinner at El Charro, a long-established landmark that served the best Mexican food I ever tasted, by far. It was located in a very dangerous neighborhood. In fact, Bruce who is a retired Tucson detective was carrying. When Bruce made a comment about his concealed weapon, Sara asked loud enough for everyone to hear, 'You have a gun with you?' The place went silent and you then heard every chair leg in the place scrape the floor, as people inched away from our table.

We stayed north of the city at Dove Mountain, location of the Tucson Ritz Carlton, and the Accenture PGA tournament. There were mountain and desert views in every direction.

On the way to Tucson, we stopped at the Wild Horse Shopping Center at the edge of the desert. It was a typical outlet mall, with all the brand name shops selling last year's merchandise at a deep, 10% discount. The store that caught my attention however, was the Dinkleberger Diamond Outlet. It got me wondering how they get their merchandise and what qualifies as an 'outlet diamond'. Did the miners dig up too many gems last month? Or did the diamond cutters have a bad day and chip too many of the diamonds? After checking the prices, the answer was apparent. Mr. Dinkleberger thinks we're all brain-dead.

Diary of a Vagabond

On Thursday, July 20, The Vagabondos left the safety of their home in Sarasota and ventured to the northern frontiers of New Jersey, New York and eventually to the eastern edge of civilization at the Outer Banks in North Carolina. It turned out to be an adventure with non-stop laughter, joy and surprises.

The first stop was Aberdeen, NJ, a town no one has ever heard of. (Actually it became a town after a fistfight at a Town Council meeting in Matawan one night.) We visited my brother John and his wife Lucille, who provided much more than food and shelter. We spent time with my nephews John and his wife Laura, and Christopher and his girlfriend, Lindsay. On Sunday, Lucille made dinner for 13 of us, including my daughter's family and my son, Ken. And she served more items than you will find on Mamma Leone's dinner menu.

But the best part of this visit was Lucille introducing us to her new make-up secret. I think it was called *Bare Naked*. She bought it on QVC (the world's longest-running infomercial). When Sara asked the cost, Lucille replied, 'Three easy payments of $29.95, plus shipping and handling.' You think she's addicted? Anyway, the stuff is so good even I tried it. You should see my cheeks! They have that au naturalle glow with no wrinkles or blemishes.

We then drove to Mahwah, NJ to stay with son Mike and Trish and our grandson, Kevin. While there, Sara took granddaughters Briana and Rita to lunch and shopping for their birthdays, while I took Kevin and Nicholas to lunch and a movie. We also attended one of Weaver's (founder of The No-Bozo Ski Adventures) famous 'Happy Hours'. It was held at a restaurant in

Saddle Brook that boasted the world's smallest parking lot. The neighbors tolerate the place, in the middle of a residential area, because of the entertainment value of watching patrons fighting over parking spots. It was a great night commiserating with about 30 of out friends, mostly from the legendary ski club.

Next day we headed to Lake George with Mike and Donna's families for a day on the lake in Mike's 20-foot Sea Ray. My son-in-law Lou and I 'topped off' the 50-gallon tank with $80 worth of gas. As Mike gunned the engine pulling out of Dunham's Bay, I turned to Lou and said, 'We just used up my share of the gas.' Dinner at Log Jam that night included a visit with Cousin Pat, the only fly-fishing, Adirondack Mountain-guiding, country swing-dancing, printing salesman in Indian Lake, NY.

Sunday morning found us heading west on the NY Thruway to visit the Geskos in Buffalo. We spent three days with them, playing golf at their beautiful country club, Wanakah that was founded in 1899. While there we had dinner at the restaurant that originated Buffalo Wings. (Of course, every bar and restaurant in the city makes that claim.) When Sara asked the hostess if we could buy a jar of their secret sauce, the woman laughed and told us to buy Frank's Hot sauce in any supermarket and mix it with butter. That's what they do. So much for that mystique. While in Buffalo, the only thing hotter than the wings was the weather. It reached into the high nineties, much hotter and more humid than Sarasota.

Returning to New Jersey, we attended a barbecue that Sara's family had at niece Joanne's house, which was attended by at least 55 people. Late in the day, everyone started singing Happy Birthday, and I looked around to see whose birthday it was. Suddenly, everyone was standing around me with a giant birthday cake that was decorated like a golf green. They were

45

surprising me with the 60th birthday party that had been cancelled at the time of the milestone. And yes, I was surprised. My sixtieth birthday had taken place 6 years, 81 days and four hours ago. But who's counting.

Following the party, we again hit the road and traveled to the Outer Banks. We spent a day with son Todd and Sue and their three daughters at the beautiful beach house they rented. While there, we heard an interesting contrast of opinions from our granddaughters on boys. While in New Jersey, Briana and Rita had described them as 'hotties.' And walking the beach in North Carolina, Amanda found them to be 'ugly, stupid and weird'.

I guess your opinion is strongly influenced by the status of your relationship at any given time.

Dodging a Bullet

OK, so they tell us that this little spot of white fuzz off the northeast coast of Africa is a potential hurricane, and it could threaten us on the west coast of Florida. At first, it doesn't even get our attention. But then as the storm organizes and they show the projected track and spaghetti models, we sat up. The weather geeks expected the hurricane to hit land between Fort Myers and Tampa. Those cities are one-hour south and north of us respectively. And that put us right in the bull's eye.

A week later on a Thursday as the storm is building in intensity, expecting to become a Category 3 hurricane (winds up to 110 mph) and is still exactly on the projected track, we decided to take action. Sara went to the store and bought a few gallons of ice cream (low carb of course) and six boxes of the new Entenmann's chewy chocolate chip cookies (high in fiber). We then removed all the potted plants from the pool cage and brought the patio furniture into the living room. Some of our neighbors actually put the furniture into the pool, but I was planning to take a swim.

On Friday morning we made our final preparations. The storm was expected to hit between 2-4 PM. In anticipation of being without water and power, we washed all the clothes and dishes, cooked hard boiled eggs, sweet potatoes (also high in fiber), took our weekly shower a day early, and filled the tub with water for drinking and flushing. I wanted to catch a tilapia or two and put them into the tub in case any mosquito larvae formed. But Sara said she wasn't drinking any water with tilapia poops in it. We then started making extra ice and set the freezer and fridge on the coldest setting so the food would go as long as possible without

47

spoiling. We also set the air conditioning on the frostbite setting and closed the vents and doors in the extra bedrooms. It got so cold in the rest of the house, we both changed to long sleeve shirts and jeans. We even charged the cell phones and the laptop. When we finished all these little tasks it was still early and the sun was shining. I decided to play golf, and I told Sara to dig a tornado shelter underneath the house while I was gone, just in case. The country club, in anticipation of golf nuts like me, had closed the course for the day.

We spoke to our friends Frank and Ruth, who live on the bank of Phillipe Creek, which was expected to surge 10 feet. Their home is 11 feet above the water level. We invited them to come and stay with us but they were too nervous about their new home furnishings. I suggested to Frank to put the new Sony big-screen Plasma TV in the car and come over. I think if we had the Yankees cable package he would have considered it. Instead, they went to the library at their clubhouse, checked out all the books, brought them home and placed them under the legs of all their furniture. They then packed the TV in the car for safe keeping, got in and drove to Orlando, where they booked a motel for two days.

So yesterday afternoon we anxiously sat in front of the TV and watched this impending monster nightmare bear down on us. We stayed in telephone contact with our friends locally to be sure we were all OK, and heard from lots of family and friends up north worried about us. Some called more than once. In fact, Harriette in Richmond, who lived through a hurricane last year, called us four times.

When the hurricane reached Ft. Myers it was upgraded to a Category 4. Winds were now at 145 mph and we were reaching high tide in most areas along the gulf coast. At this intensity the hurricane was expected to surge the gulf waters up to 17 feet above the high tide mark. (New homes along the gulf are built 12 feet above high tide.)

The storm was projected to veer east at some point, because of the low-pressure trough that had recently carried Hurricane Bonnie up the coast. It was expected that it would turn into Lemon Bay (Fort Myers), or Tampa Bay. Tampa being the largest bay by far and according to the spaghetti models, the most likely. Surprisingly, the storm abruptly turned up the bay at Port Charlotte, which is south of us, and headed inland. This was good news for us as it now put us on the weakest side of the storm center and no longer a storm surge threat. However, the hurricane was now headed in an unexpected direction where people were least prepared. It was also bearing down on shelters, homes and hotels where evacuees from the barrier islands had gone for safety.

As the storm went up Charlotte Harbor, we began to feel the strong winds and heavy rain. After about an hour the eye of the hurricane, still packing 120 mph winds passed within 20 miles of our home. When you realize that the storm was 350 miles wide, in both the Gulf and the Atlantic at the same time, this was as close to a direct hit as you can get. Ruth and Frank were now in the bull's eye of the storm and their motel in Orlando quickly lost power and suffered external damage to the building. But by some miracle, the big flat screen TV was undamaged by the hurricane.

We were very fortunate in that our neighborhood fell between the intense storm bands that the hurricane spins off. We got less than an inch of rain (other areas got 8 inches) and wind gusts never exceeded 70 mph. In the end we had one flowering tree fall over and no other damage. And then it was gone. And it's a good thing, because Sara never finished digging the shelter.

This morning we're watching the aftermath on TV and counting our blessings. But then the weather geek just showed us another spot of white fuzz off the coast of Africa, right where the last one was.

Extreme Golf

After an enjoyable round of golf the other day, I went up to the lounge in our clubhouse to enjoy a drink with the other players. From the lounge, you have a panoramic view of the course, and from where we sat we could watch the golfers play the 18th hole.

A group was teeing off and we saw three of them land their ball safely in the middle of the fairway. The fourth golfer sliced his shot badly, landing in a bunker on the far right of the fairway. From that position, the green is on the left side, 160 yards away with a stiff wind coming from the back of the green across the fairway. There is also a lake between the narrow fairway and the green, plus sand traps and moguls guarding it, making for an extremely difficult second shot even under ideal conditions.

As this golfer approached the sand bunker, I could tell from his body language that he was not having a good day. Under the circumstances, the prudent choice in this situation is to take a short, easy lay-up out of the bunker and let the ball roll towards the lake. Then take a shot to the green and try to land close to the pin. From where we sat, we couldn't tell what club the golfer selected, but I guessed that he was using a long iron, and going for the green. I figured if he made this nearly impossible shot and reached the green, it would encourage him to return to play another day. I guessed right. The golfer took a huge swing and with an explosion of sand we watched the ball loft into the air and land in the middle of the lake.

The dejected golfer drove his cart to the edge of the lake, dropped a ball and prepared for his next shot, which was only about 50 yards. After standing over the ball for a long time (too long), he took another hellish swing, nearly coming out of his shoes, to be sure this shot made it over the lake and onto the green. The massive divot he took, which was the size of an area throw rug, actually went further than the ball and it nearly made it over the lake. As we were sitting in the lounge, feeling this guy's pain, his playing partner was trying to calm him down. Obviously, his partner stood to loose a lot of money on the outcome of the match. Our enraged golfer, then dropped another ball, took a few deep breaths and prepared to take another shot. This time, he swung easy, probably following his partner's advice. The shot was just a little too easy, and it hit the bank on the far side, rolling back into the lake.

No human being can be expected to deal with this kind of pain and frustration. So when the golfer flung his club into the lake, no one was surprised. The surprise came, however, when he calmly walked back to the cart, took his pricey, leather tournament bag full of expensive golf clubs and threw it into the lake. He then stormed off the course, leaving his cart at the edge of the lake, and his bewildered friends behind. At this point, we were no longer feeling pain or compassion, we were howling in the lounge, along with a considerable crowd that had gathered to witness this devastation. Each one secretly thinking, 'There, but for the grace of God. . .'

After about five minutes, our golfer friend returned to the scene of the crime, obviously having second thoughts about his compulsive behavior. (We estimated that it was about a $2,500 temper tantrum.) He removed his shoes and socks and then threw about a dozen golf balls into the lake, apparently trying to scare off any alligators (alligators love toes). He then waded out, waist deep into the lake, feeling around the muck with his feet until he found the golf bag. He lifted it out of the water, opened a zippered pocket, removed his car keys and then threw the bag even further into the lake. He then got out of the lake, sat in the cart, retrieved a towel from the basket, and dried himself off. And then he put on his shoes and socks. We recognized that he had now recovered and was back to normal. But he had one more surprise. Standing alongside the cart, he reached in with his foot, released the brake and tapped the accelerator, as the cart rolled down the embankment and became partially submerged in the lake.

At that point, I was certain that he wasn't coming into the lounge for a drink.

Horse Trading

After we returned from Lake Tahoe and Sara's knee surgery from the skiing accident, her friend took her to the orthopedic surgeon for her checkup. (I was at another doctor's appointment) After the exam, she got the news she was hoping for. He said she can start putting weight on the broken leg and begin walking. However, he was prescribing six weeks of rehab. When she got up to take a step, she nearly fell down, but by leaning on a crutch, she was now able to walk!

She was so excited that when her friend dropped her off at home, she drove her new car for the first time. She went to a wine shop and bought a bottle of champagne to celebrate. On the way home, she decided to take a ride in the country. (We live on the edge of civilization in Florida.) While driving along this one lane road, she came upon a woman walking down the road, carrying two large bags. Sara stopped and offered the woman a ride. It turned out that she was a Seminole Indian. And this was probably the first native Floridian Sara had met down here.

The woman sat in the passenger seat and didn't say anything, but kept looking at the paper bag with the champagne. Finally, to break the silence, Sara said, 'I got it for my husband.'

The Indian lady replied, 'Good trade.'

How to Survive a Hurricane

All of the hurricane activity this year has had so many of our friends and family calling and emailing to see if we are OK. In fact, some of the more emotional calls have been to urge us to move back north. After considering that advice, we have made a commitment that the day Hurricane Zachary hits the Florida Coast we will call the movers. We recognize that it would not be any safer in New Jersey, especially considering the blizzards, toxic waste sites, air pollution, road rage, drive-by shootings and death by taxation.

But everyone, please relax as we are fine here. Now that we're seeing one hurricane a week, we've become really good at preparing for them. As the third major storm of the year threatened our area, we, along with our friends took appropriate steps. Let me share those critical activities with you.

As I explained in a previous email, as a storm approaches, Sara runs to the supermarket to stock up on comfort food. She will buy Double Dutch Chocolate ice cream, sweetened with Splenda, Entenmann's new low net carb chocolate chip cookies and a large jar of Nutella, that decadent hazelnut chocolate spread that you heap on Italian bread. I'm sure you're wondering how this shopping list qualifies as comfort food, so let me ask you? Did you ever see a skinny person who looked comfortable?

A couple of days prior to Ivan's arrival, my friend Bruce, who just moved here from Tucson with his wife Marianne, borrowed my power washer. He decided to pressure clean his walkways. I guess he wanted to make a good impression on the FEMA field reps that determine who gets the government disaster relief checks.

Our other friend Frank, who readily admits he doesn't handle stress well, went into action as soon as word was out that Ivan could possibly hit the west coast of Florida. At the time it was still an unnamed tropical depression somewhere off the west coast of Africa. He immediately booked airline tickets to New Jersey, so he and his wife Ruth would be out of town when the storm arrived. Ironically, his scheduled flight coincided with the arrival of the remnants of Hurricane Frances as it reached the Garden State. Even more ironic, the return date that he booked would have him back in Sarasota just as Ivan was to arrive (after it slowed down and caused the weather geniuses to change their forecasts twelve times).

My other friend Tom (who moved here from California with his wife Susie) had the best idea of all. After dodging two bullets, he figured our number was up with Ivan, so he decided to fortify his house and hunker down. He went to Home Depot and got on line with the other 200 handymen who got there just before he did. He purchased 30 sheets of plywood at $15 a pop, a $129 Skil Saw, a Black & Decker screw gun for $69 and $120 worth of lag screws and concrete drill bits.

Tom went home and measured and cut pieces to fit every one of the 21 windows, sliders and doors in his house. He then invited Bruce and Marianne, Frank and Ruth (by this time, they had cancelled their plans to skip town), and Sara and me to ride out the hurricane inside his sealed tomb. The only catch was, that us guys had to help drill the holes in the stucco/cement block walls and screw on the plywood panels. Knowing how difficult it is to drill concrete, I volunteered to run the screw crew. Since the storm kept slowing down, we kept delaying the installation of the panels. Finally, we decided that we would call a board meeting Sunday morning to determine if that would be the big day. At 7 AM Sunday morning, I checked the weather and realized that Ivan was probably going to miss us, and at most we would get a deluge of rain. As chairman of the screw committee, I called Tom the board chairman, and advised him that we were staging a work stoppage. He conferred with the other directors and the vote was unanimous. With the work cancelled, we all went to the beach.

So now you know how Florida veterans prepare for a hurricane. Oh, I didn't tell you how I prepared for the hurricane. Realizing that this killer storm would most likely dump several inches of rain on us, I decided to get in some golf before the course was washed out. So while we screwed around deciding if we should screw the boards, I played three rounds.

Love Bugs

We just survived another life and death experience in Florida: The annual invasion of the love bugs. These innocuously named creatures seem to have no beneficial purpose in life. They look like fireflies, but instead of glowing in the dark, they just crowd your space all day long. When they hatch, there are dozens of them per square foot, creating a nuisance, as I will describe below.

As they emerge into the world, they immediately seek the companionship of the opposite sex. Hence "love bugs." The smaller male attaches himself to his larger female mate, tail to tail and they fly around with her in the lead and him in tow. Sara assumes that she leads because he's afraid to ask for directions. When I first saw them in the air, it reminded me of a comment made by an irate divorcée at a singles forum many years ago. She got up in front of hundreds of eligible men and women and angrily proclaimed, 'Men are emotional cripples, that have to be lead around by the penis!' At the time, I dismissed the comment as having no basis in fact. Now I have reason to believe otherwise. But I'm digressing.

You can't imagine the mess these little buggers make. A short trip to the grocery store leaves your windshield, bumper, and hood covered with hundreds of crushed bodies, embraced to each other and baked on to your car by the sun. Bike riding is even more difficult. They're on your arms, legs and chest, procreating away. If you open your mouth, they perceive it as a tunnel of love. And you certainly don't want that happening in your mouth!

These plague-like swarms are an amazing thing to see. Hundreds of thousands of them are in the air, wandering aimlessly in search of some unknown destination. The female is doing all the work, pulling the male along backwards in their love ritual. What he thinks is erotic ecstasy is actually airsickness. And when they splatter on your windshield, what you think is love serum is really his lunch.

Pooping in Paradise

Continuing our tradition of not going more than a few weeks without houseguests, last week we had a visit from Sara's niece Margie and our longtime friend Lillian. Unlike previous visitors, these women were regular Jo's in every way imaginable. You see, whenever we have guests stay with us, we force them to eat healthy. You won't find saturated fats, high sugar or high carb products in our house, just sensible, healthy food to make it easy to maintain weight. This kind of a diet is such a shock on the digestive systems of most of our guests that they immediately become constipated. Well, not these two Jo's. Because they're so regular, the first morning the toilet bowl became clogged as a result of their active biological functions. You see the toilet bowl had become so complacent from lack of use that it rebelled against all this pressure. The plunger, which had begun to rot from disuse, broke when we tried to unclog the bowl.

But Margie and Lillian were regular in other ways, as well. Rather than arriving with a sense of adventure, they came with their plans and itineraries prepared and their to-do list complete. Margie wanted to spend all sunlit hours at the beach, see some condos and go barhopping. (She thought that if she got Lillian into some bars, she would meet Mr. Right and Margie's purpose in life would be fulfilled). Lillian, on the other hand, wanted to play lots of golf, and play we did. While none of us scored well, we had fun, and cursed, played lots of courses and cursed, and hit the ball too many times and cursed (too many times).

Margie did get to see some housing, two to be exact. Sara took her to see a condo that is selling for $130,000 and one that is over $1 million. Well, at least she now knows the price range.

On Saturday night, we went to the bar that was voted Best in Sarasota. It's a martini bar called Fred's. Most of the girls ordered French martinis, which the bartender didn't know how to make, and the rest of us (we were nine altogether) ordered cappuccino martinis, chocolate martinis and cookie dough martinis (oops, I think that was the ice cream shop order). Tom was the only sensible one and he ordered a Kettle One straight up with an olive, kinda like James Bond. Being the cosmopolitan sophisticate that I am, I ordered a Sloe Gin Fizz.

The highlight of the week was a picnic on Siesta Beach to watch the sunset on Sunday evening. Every Sunday at the beach, there is a sunset ritual, where a disorganized band of renegades and misfits shows up and starts playing bongo drums and other assorted 'instruments'. This always attracts a crowd of guys wearing thongs and Puca shells, beards and pony tails, just like the Sixties, except that they are all in their sixties. The women that the event draws are mostly uninhibited exhibitionists, belly dancing and swaying to the irregular beat. And then there is the large crowd of people watchers. We went to watch the people watchers watching the eclectic entertainers. For example, there was one executive type gentleman, wearing expensive clothes. He brought his "niece" who was sporting abundant breast implants addition to her well-sculpted body. They were talking to a young guy who had a ten-foot boa constrictor wrapped around his neck and shoulders. The snake was obviously attracted to the 'niece' as he immediately began wrapping himself around her curves. I learned later that this boa was raised on melons.

Well, before you knew it, the sun was setting, our dinner of whole-wheat wraps was finished and the wine was gone. Also, the fragrant cloud hanging above the circle of drummers and entertainers began to drift out over the Gulf. It was time to pack our beach chairs and make our way off the Key and over to Sweetberries, a special frozen custard store, where God goes for his ice cream.

Of course, ingesting all that lactose triggered another rush to the bathroom. But by now the, the toilet bowl had gotten used to the two regular Jo's, so it was a non-event.

Snow Job

Oct. 14 - New Jersey in the fall is the most beautiful place on earth. The leaves are turning all different colors - you should see the beautiful shades of red and orange and yellow! We went for a ride through an area of gorgeous rolling hills and spotted some deer. They are so graceful, and certainly they are the most peaceful animals on earth. This must be Paradise. I love it here!

Nov. 3 - Deer season will start soon. I can't imagine anyone wanting to kill such an elegant creature, the very symbol of peace and tranquility. I hope it will snow soon. I love it here!

Dec. 2 - It snowed last night! Woke up to find everything blanketed in white, just like a postcard. We went outside and cleaned the snow off the steps and shoveled the driveway. We had a snowball fight (I won) and when the snowplow came by, we had to shovel the front of driveway again. What a beautiful place. Mother nature is in perfect harmony. I love New Jersey!

Dec. 12 - More snow last night. I love it. The snowplow did his trick again (that rascal) and pushed all the snow back into the driveway, but we bundled up and had a good time clearing it - and we made a snowman out of it! It's a winter wonderland. I love it here!

Dec. 19 - More snow last night. Couldn't get out of the driveway to get to work on time! I'm exhausted from shoveling. Yep. That damn snowplow again!

Dec. 22 - More of that white crap fell last night. I've got blisters on my hands from shoveling. I think the snowplow man hides around the corner and waits until I'm done shoveling this driveway, the jerk! And you should see our heating bills!

Dec. 25 - "White Christmas" my busted ass! We got more friggin' snow. If I ever get my hands on that son of a bitch who drives that snowplow, I swear I'll break the bastard's nose. Don't know why they don't use more salt on the roads to melt this friggin ICE!

Dec. 28 – The shit keeps coming. More last night. Been inside since Christmas Day except for shoveling out the driveway every time 'Snowplow Sammy comes by. Can't go anywhere, car's buried in a mountain of frozen snow. The weatherman says to expect another 10" of the shit tonight. Do you know how many shovels full of snow 10" is?

Jan. 1 - Happy Damn New Year, the weatherman was wrong AGAIN. We got two feet of the white shit this time. At this rate it won't melt before the Fourth of July. The snowplow got stuck up the road, and the jerk had the balls to come to my door and ask to borrow my shovel. After I told him I've broken six shovels already, shoveling all the crap he pushed into the driveway, I broke my last one over his damn head!

Jan. 8 - Finally got out of the house today. Went to the store to get food and on the way back, a damn deer ran in front of the car and I hit the bastard. Did about $3,000 worth of damage to the car. Those damn beasts ought to be eradicated. Wish the hunters had killed them all last November.

Mar. 22 - Took the car to the garage in town. Would you believe the thing is rotting out from all that damn salt they keep dumping all over the road? Car looks like a piece of shit! Also noticed that the deer have been eating all the flower buds, so no roses, azaleas and hibiscus this year again. Insatiable bastards!

April. 1 - Moved back to Florida. I can't imagine why anyone in their right mind would ever want to live in that God forsaken state of New Jersey!

The Cariddi Dialogs

For the last two weeks, my in-laws Tommy and Lisa spent a vacation with us and it was non-stop bantering between them. It was the best entertainment we had all year. Our friends were hysterical.

(On the Beach)

'My God, look at the size of the ass on her.' 'Those are the fattest legs I've seen all week.' 'That one's got no chest at all.'

'Tommy, do you have to say something negative about everybody you see? You're not so hot yourself.'

'Lisa, be quiet.'

(At Home after the Beach)

'Tommy, your face is all red. You got sunburned. Why didn't you wear sunblock?'

'Lisa, you don't know nothing. I'm not sunburned.'

'Go look in the mirror. You're all red.'

'Lisa, it's from the wind. Why don't you be quiet?'

(In the Restaurant)

'Tommy, you're having more bread? Look at the size of your stomach.'

'Lisa, look at your own stomach. You can't even fit into your clothes.'

'Don't eat so much bread. Save room for ice cream later.'

(Later in the Week)

'Boy Lisa, this beach is Paradise. This beach is better than Aruba. It's Paradise.'

'Tommy, how many times are you going to say it? You always repeat yourself.'

'Lisa, you don't know what you're talking about. Why don't you just be quiet?'

(Dinner at Home)

'Lisa, be quiet.'

But Tommy, I'm telling a story about Italy.'

'How many times are you going to tell that same story?'

'But, they never heard this story.

'Boy, one drink and you can't stop talking. Why don't you shove this (napkin) in your mouth for a couple of hours.'

(At the Country Club)

'Tommy, I love to dance. You never want to dance.'

'Lisa, I dance at every wedding.'

'What. One slow dance? You promised to take dancing lessons when we got married.'

'What are you talking about? I know how to dance. I dance when I want. And besides, that was 50 years ago.'

(In the Kitchen)

'Tommy, you cleaned up Sara's refrigerator. Why don't you do the pantry for her?'

'Sara's pantry is just fine. I'll do it before we leave.'

'Don't straighten it out too much. She'll have trouble finding things.'

'Lisa, you can't find nothing. Just drink your wine and be quiet.'

(In the family room)

'Tommy, why don't we get a computer so we can read Mike's emails?'

'Lisa, I'm 73 years old. I'm not getting no computer.'

(Before leaving for the Airport)

'Come on Lisa, let's go.'

'Why did you get me up so early? The plane doesn't leave for six hours.'

'I want to get to the airport early. I don't want no stress.'

'What are we going to do at the airport for over three hours?'

'We'll have breakfast and look at the people. Now be quiet and get ready.'

Wheelchair Adventure

Yesterday I brought Sara to the orthopedic surgeon to have the staples removed from her six-inch incision. Boy was that fun. He told us that she is making good progress and she should begin bending the knee immediately. In another week or so, she can get in the pool and start swimming. This should really help the atrophy problem. And in four weeks, she should be able to start putting weight on it.

Following the doctor's visit, I took her to an estate furniture store (used household junk) where they have a paperback book exchange. While Sara searched the bookshelves, I found a pair of used crutches hanging on a wall. Being the big shot that I am, I sprung for the $8.00 they wanted for the crutches. (I'm trying to find out if I can put in an insurance claim for them.) These are added to the walker we bought in Lake Tahoe for $144 and the wheelchair I scored for $75. All I need now is a gurney and we have transportation for any situation.

I should tell you about Sara's wheelchair adventure. She asked me to help her into the garage so she could go through the recycle bin to locate an article in the newspaper that I discarded before she read it. So I wheeled her out there and then went back into my office to do some work. A minute later, I heard the car horn blowing and I got annoyed because she could have knocked on the back door instead of letting the entire neighborhood know that she had found the article.

Actually, that was not the case. When she stood up to pull some newspapers out of the bin, the wheelchair rolled backwards out of the garage, down the driveway and across the street, leaving her stranded in the middle of the garage. Somehow she hobbled on one foot to the car and summoned me.

These little inconveniences are minor, compared to her anxiety to get back on the golf course, now that the weather has gotten more seasonal. In an effort to overcome her frustration, I've been creating a new version of golf, just for people like Sara. It's called GOLO. What I do is strap Sara into the driver's seat of our golf cart and she drives it as fast as she can across the fairways and hits the ball with a seven iron. She repeats this until the ball goes in the cup. The beauty part of this version of the game is that you don't have to worry about avoiding horse droppings. The only drawback so far is that we've destroyed all the greens on the golf course trying to perfect the game. In fact, the club management is threatening to revoke my membership. This may force us to shift gears and try Wheelchair Gockey.

Wine Tasting Extravaganza

While working outside their new home a couple of weeks ago, our friends Bluffy and Boney Whiner met the neighbors across the street. As a welcoming gesture, the Blasés invited them to a wine tasting party they were hosting on Saturday evening. It seems that Randy, the husband, studied wine at Cal Davis. When Bluffy explained that they had plans with us for that date, Randy said, "Bring them along. We're expecting about 50 people."

So this past Saturday we went to pick up the Whiners and go across the street to the wine tasting. Bluffy and Boney offered us a drink before we left, but we declined, expecting to be over-served at the party. Bluffy was telling us that Randy had worked like a mule all day getting the outside of the house ready for the party. He hired some 14 year-old kid to cut the lawn and use a machete to cut down the dead branches on the overgrown shrubs. This was an obvious violation of OSHA regulations, not to mention the child labor laws. Meantime, Randy literally ran around the house with a commercial edger, motor running full bore, to edge the walkways and beds. While he and the kid were doing the lawn work, his own two sons played basketball in the driveway. This must have been frustrating, as when we walked up the driveway that evening, it was still covered with grass cuttings.

We were greeted at the door by one of the sons and directed us into the kitchen, where all 54 guests were crammed around the counter. The counter top was packed with appetizers (we were all asked to bring a bottle of wine or two, and an appetizer). It was apparent that most of the people there were creative thinkers, because about two thirds of them brought a cheese platter. Actually platter is not accurate, saucer would be more appropriate. For the most part the guests matched the Blasés in charm, wit and intellect. And fortunately, there were also a few really interesting people there, as well. One guy, who was a runner-up for the Nobel Prize in Demographics, tried to convince me that all the baby-boomers who were going to retire to Florida were already here. The other 50 million won't be able to afford to retire. One guy introduced himself to Bluffy and said that he was the Misty Creek real estate agent. When Bluffy introduced himself, the guy said, 'Oh, you bought your house from Cathy Carbone, the agent at Saunders who also lives in Misty Creek.' Before Bluffy could say yes, the guy turned and walked away.

Among the guests were a charming couple from Mexico City, who brought the best appetizers, something spicy and cheesy with a name I can't pronounce. And a couple from New Zealand, brought some terrific wines that you can't get in the USA. Speaking of wines, except for the New Zealand bottles, most of them were as memorable as the cheese saucers, but I'm getting ahead. You have to picture 50 people standing on one side of the counter looking at all this food and the Blasés on the other side of the counter looking confused, but unconcerned. Since there were no dishes or utensils, no one touched the food. And since it was a wine tasting, we were waiting for Randy to kick off the tasting part of the evening. After we stood around for half an hour, Bluffy leaned over and said to me, 'I bet you wish you had that drink at our place before we came here.'

At about that time Randy began to gather all the white wine and put the bottles in a large tub full of ice. He also brought all the red wine into the dining room and set them on the table. About an hour into the party, people just couldn't take it any more, so they started to pick on the appetizers (the Kraft and Velveeta cheeses were getting mushy). Within 20 minutes most of the food was eaten, at least all the good stuff was gone. An hour and forty-five after we arrived, Randy began his lecture on wine, in which he explained that tasting wine was an individual thing, and you shouldn't pay attention to ratings. End of lecture.

Then he opened the first bottle of wine. He started with the white, and opened the cheapest bottle first, and then only a couple at a time. As bad as these wines were, there was a stampede to the table to get some, as we were dying of thirst. After an hour of white, and only one bottle worth tasting, the entertainment portion of the evening began. (Actually I found the entire evening to be entertaining, but that was not the intent.) One guest wearing black leather pants (it was ninety degrees outside) began playing the piano in the living room and his date started singing. Everyone now migrated into the living room, partly because of the singing and partly because the kitchen temperature had reached the outside temperature. (I think Randy had the air conditioning programmed to shut off at 7 PM.) One woman complained about the heat and I explained that it wasn't the heat. It was the humanity. Anyway, our talented singer began to belt it out with her big soprano voice, much too big for the tiny living room that was decorated in early clutter and neo trash. Her finale was a song from Phantom that would give Sarah Brightman a run for her money.

Now it was time to drink the red wine, and Randy opened a couple of bottles, explaining that they should breathe awhile. It was now 10 PM and people were leaving, so breathing be damned, the remaining crowd started inhaling the red wine. We were fortunate to taste some of the New Zealand Shiraz and a couple of other interesting reds before they were gone, and then we left the party both hungry and thirsty. Sara commented to Boney that the Blasés plan was to have a party, collect a lot of wine, serve the stuff that tasted like cleaning fluid, and add the good stuff to their own supply.

The Whiners were gracious enough to invite us in to their house for dessert, because we would have had to wait until sunrise to have some at the Blasés.

Golf - A Life and Death Struggle

Golf is supposed to be good for your health. Doctors recommend it to recovering heart attack victims. It's a chance to be outdoors, breathing fresh air and getting some sunshine. It involves a lot of walking and other forms of exercise, and if you don't get too intense, it can be very relaxing. But when you hear words like hazard, trap, handicap, stroke, and bunker, you have to wonder, 'Just how safe is golf?'

Well, if you play the public courses, there are some real dangers to consider. First you could die of boredom waiting for the group in front of you to get off the green. Then, of course you must always beware of the errant shot, which could come from anywhere, including your playing partner. People forget to yell *Fore!* (They especially forget seven, eight and nine, when they're keeping score.) Once I was standing ten feet off the side of the tee watching my partner's tee shot. It missed my head by inches. I still don't know how he could hit it that hard, sideways. Another time, I was on the tee hitting my own drive when I struck the ball too low. It hit the tee marker on the ladies tee, ricocheting back past my ear and landed in a lake fifty yards behind me. So I'm now laying three and I haven't gotten past the ladies' tee yet.

Another hazard is flying golf clubs. Often, when a golfer loses his temper, he throws his club, as if it were the club's fault that he shanked his shot into the woods. I've seen $400 drivers land in trees and not come down. (But better in the trees than between my eyes.) Then the player has to throw other expensive clubs into the tree hoping the driver comes out and the other clubs don't become part of a condor's nest.

Some people like to live on a golf course. I guess they like to listen to colorful language, starting at six am. The problem is, that when you sit on you lanai, you have to wear artillery helmets and Kevlar vests. It's like dining al fresco in Baghdad.

The other really dangerous thing about golf is lightning. You know the saying, 'You have a better chance of winning the lottery than being hit by lightning.' Well, if you're a golfer, your chances of being struck go up dramatically. And if you play golf in Florida, the odds actually move in your favor. The Tampa area gets more lightning strikes than anywhere in the world, except some obscure village in Africa, where they have no golfers, not anymore. Lightning is attracted to open areas, trees and water. Sure sounds like a golf course, right? Within the last few months in the Sarasota-Manatee area, just south of Tampa, two golfers died and four others have been hospitalized by lightning strikes, and nobody's won the lottery there. Makes you wonder.

Behavior Modification

For over 10 years, I have been playing golf with a group of guys that are more focused on fun than handicap. During that time the number of regulars has grown from four to over 20. Of course, when you think of the number of rounds played you can understand why we know each other's quirks, blemishes and warts.

Take my friend Frank, for instance. He is Mr. Tranquility. Frank has a soft-spoken voice, calm demeanor, and he never loses his temper. Except of course, on the golf course. Frank is a good athlete, but a poor golfer, so he gets frustrated easily because the game does not come easily for him.

Recently, we organized a couples outing for all the guys and their wives. And as soon as we announced it, Frank's wife called me up and advised me that she has discontinued playing golf with him. She can't take his rants, tantrums, constant outpouring of F-bombs, and his dangerous throwing of his golf clubs. I hadn't played in Frank's foursome in a while, so I found Ruth's description shocking. I asked a few of the other golfers, and they shared the same experience. Giving Frank the benefit of the doubt, I concluded that the dosage of his meds had to be off. I called Ruth and she told me that he had actually increased his dosage, especially on the days he played golf.

Fearing that Frank might hurt himself, I devised a plan for the next week's golf game. I arranged for Frank to play with me, and one of the other golfers from the group. I also invited my friend Uwe to join the foursome. Since Frank had never met Uwe, my plan had a good chance of success. When we got to the first tee, I introduced everyone to 'Father Uwe'. He solemnly bowed and thanked us all for letting him join us. He also made the sign of the cross, giving us his blessing. Frank rode with me that day, and he immediately asked me if Father Uwe was really a priest. I replied, 'You'd better act like St. Francis, and don't you dare embarrass me in front of the good reverend.'

The game (and the plan) went smashingly well. Uwe played the part perfectly. Every time he made a good shot, he threw a kiss to Heaven. Frank, for his part was the model golfer. Every time he made a bad shot, which was constantly, he tightened up, scrunched his face, squeezed the club's grip, and took a deep breath. All was going great.

And then on the 17th hole, Uwe sliced his drive way into the woods. He banged his club into the ground and screamed, 'This fucking game is madness! The godless bastard from Scotland who invented it, should spend eternity in Hell with his fucking balls burning on a hot skillet.'

Frank stood there in shock. And the three of us laughed so hard, we couldn't finish the round. And that's when Frank started unleashing his string of F-bombs and other expletives that he had withheld the entire round.

Alligator Allie

Our friends from around the country are all contacting us, concerned for our welfare while we are here in Florida. Watching the national news has everyone convinced that we're in a life-and-death struggle with an exploding alligator population. Well, I'm glad to say we're just fine. Actually, it's the alligators that are in danger. No, the Red Tide isn't getting them and neither is the pesticides leaching into the water from our lawns. It's another outbreak of Severe Media Frenzy.

It all started with some of the local newspaper editors skipping their medication. And then at a national convention of headline writers, a group of college kids slipped some concentrated Hysteria into the water supply. Right after the writers got back to work (on a slow news day), three women in separate incidents were attacked by alligators, making the perfect storm of journalism.

First, let me tell you about the attacks. One woman went snorkeling at dusk, which is feeding time for gators, presenting herself as dinner. The second woman sat on a low trestle bridge dangling her feet inches above the waterline. We all know alligators love toes, so she was a goner, feet first, so to speak. The third woman, Allie, was luckier. She was watering her flowers when a gator mistook her hose for a snake and went after it. She whacked him in the snout with the nozzle and he took off. The other non-story contributing to the hype is about all the pets that are disappearing. Again, this is being blamed on your friendly neighborhood alligator. The press, of course, ignores the fact that pets will travel thousands of miles to return to their original home. And they have also been ignoring all the dogs and cats that are walking along I 75 on their way back to Ohio.

And now, every time some lovable alligator pops his head out of the water and gives someone a toothy smile, they panic and call the Alligator Police. My buddy Al, who is a licensed trapper, has been pulling about 20 gators a day out of the lakes. The TV crews are eating it up, filming Al at every chance. You've probably seen him on TV or on the Internet. One IQ-challenged anchor breathlessly told the TV audience that Al was so busy during this alligator insurgency that he had a backlog of 39 sightings to respond to. I quickly did the math and that came out to two day's work. Wow!

At this rate, unless some real news distracts the press, the Florida alligators will soon make the Endangered Species list. With mosquitoes now almost non-existent in Florida, the only pests left will be the over-the-top news reporters. And of course, the snowbirds.

Gas Pains

That pain that's roiling through your stomach is not indigestion. It's gas. Just thinking about spending fifty bucks a tankful is giving everybody *agita*. A lot of people are faced with a difficult choice, deciding whether to spend money on gas or buy food. Well this might be a good time to start that diet you promised to go on, back in January. While some people have started to cut back on their food shopping, I don't see anyone drinking less bottled water. That still costs several times the price of gas, even at today's prices. At a buck and a half a bottle, it comes to $12 a gallon . . . for water!

Although most people are standing around wringing their hands and complaining about gas prices, I decided to do something about it. I did some research that I would like to share with you to help you better manage the cost of driving. The following are some gas-saving ideas that you can put to use immediately. You'll find these a lot easier than selling the monster truck and buying a hybrid.

First, some vacation tips. When you go to New Hampshire this year, don't bring your mother-in-law. The reduction in weight will save you big time, especially when you climb Mt. Washington. Also, forget the speedboat this year. At eight gallons an hour, you'll go broke in one weekend. Take the family kayaking. And bring your mother-in-law. She'll be speechless.

And some driving tips. Don't believe all those reports that driving fast uses more gas. It's bunk. The faster you're going, the longer you can coast, especially downhill. And that's when you rack up great miles per gallon. Gas mileage goes down when you use your brakes, so avoid using them at all cost. And remember, red lights are merely a suggestion, continue to run through them, as stopping cuts your fuel efficiency. And make sure your horn is working. It will help keep pedestrians out of the crosswalks when you're driving through downtown. Always take the most direct route to your destination, even if this means driving up one-way streets, across lawns or through construction sites. We're in an emergency situation here.

All of these tips will help you cope with the shift in spending, but they are only band-aid solutions. Unfortunately, the future does not look good for affordable gas prices. The Mid-east sheiks and mullahs are getting too used to the extra income, so expect high prices to be permanent. For the long term, you better consider buying one of those fuel-efficient sub-compacts. Last week a young, car-loving couple was forced to make that tough choice in order to start their marriage off on sound financial footing. The day before the wedding, the groom, convinced he was doing the right thing took the painful step. He traded in his full-size Nissan sedan for a two-door Cooper. His disappointed bride lamented, 'In just one day, he went from a Maxi to a Mini. And I thought he was going to surprise me on my wedding night with a Hummer!'

In a Mexican Minute

We just returned from a vacation in Mexico. It was our first trip there and it made us wonder why Mexicans are risking their lives to come to America to do grunt work for five bucks an hour. Our destination was Cabo San Lucas, a tiny village at the very end of the Baja Peninsula. The terrain is starkly beautiful, while the Pacific Ocean and Sea of Cortez are dazzlingly brilliant. The shoreline of both these bodies of water are lined with opulent resorts and impeccable golf courses. And we found the people to be happy and friendly.

The weather was great (85 degrees and dry), and the pace is slow, painfully slow. A half-hour lunch in the grill-room of the Cabo Del Sol golf course took one and a half hours, and we nearly missed our tee time. In order to get to play the golf course at a reasonable cost, we had to sit through a 75-minute presentation on their timeshare program. The sales pitch, which actually lasted three hours and fifteen minutes, saved us nearly $175 off the $275 greens fee. And no, we didn't buy our piece of the Hacienda Resort.

Getting any service in a reasonable amount of time is a major challenge in Mexico. It is second only to getting accurate information. On the golf adventure, we were told that the presentation started at 8:30 AM. However, it began at 9:15. The presentation lasted two hours longer than advertised. Our 1:30 tee time abruptly became 2:30. Without explanation, the $85 discounted greens fees became $110. The advertised 'finest three finishing holes in golf' had one hole that wasn't finished. (We played to a temporary green.)

Fishing wasn't much better. We booked a charter boat for a half day's fishing. Since we were eight people, the price was $650 for a 38-foot boat ($450 for a 36 foot boat, if only six of us went) including licenses, bottled water, bait, etc. When the eight of us arrived at the dock the next morning, the boat had shrunk to 36 foot but the price was still $650, and suddenly all of us could fit. And there was a $10 per person charge for licenses and $10 for bait. The one 12 oz. bottle of water in the on-board cooler was still free.

'Quality Standards' and 'simple logic' are oxymorons in Mexico. In many cases and for no apparent reason, sidewalks within a one-block stretch vary from street level to a few feet above the roadbed. This of course, requires steps for pedestrians. The first step might be three inches high, the second, eight inches and the top step could be 16 inches high. And the width of the steps varied wildly as well. Every street is lined with speed bumps. In a quarter mile stretch, you could encounter a bump three feet wide and three inches high, and the next one will be one foot wide and eight inches high. Buses (salvaged school buses, no longer considered safe or usable in the US) approach these bumps at one to two miles per hour lest the wheels fall off, while the loco locals in their dusty pick-ups take them at 40 mph. The handicap ramps at the hotel, which average about a 35-degree pitch, all have signs, 'For Employees Only'. The room staff spends hours fan-folding the ends of the toilet paper and the tissue that sticks out of the box, but they neglect to sweep the dust and debris behind the bathroom door. Every morning, they spend two hours hand-rolling the beach area in front of the hotel rooms (an area about the size of four football fields) with lead pipes, removing every footprint. Then they walk back across the sand to retrieve their shirts.

And the unions are worried that the Mexicans are going to take American jobs?

A Golfer's Cry for Help

The Plea

Dear Master Professional,

Former 10-index, injury-prone, aging golfer, with delicate ego, lack of confidence, and suicidal tendencies is in dire need of help. Subject is in possession of brand-new, brand name, custom made golf clubs specified to fit his pathetic swing. If you are up for the challenge of providing a simple tune-up lesson and possibly some psychiatric consultation, you will be assured of a fascinating case study.

Respond directly to the victim with soonest available appointment times. Confidentiality is required.

Desperately,

Michael Sisti

The Response

Dear Desperate,

Recognizing your need and the potential for self-inflicted harm, I have adjusted my schedule and set aside my very first appointment tomorrow morning for a one-hour lesson. And from the description of your situation, I'll hold open the second hour, as well.

Brad Myers

Certified PGA Master Professional

The Confirmation

Thank you, Mr. Myers. I will be there early tomorrow morning. I'm sure I will only need a half hour. After all, I've been a low handicap golfer for years, and I'm well versed on swing mechanics. I don't need you to change my swing. I just need a little tweak.

And of all the golf pros out there, I picked you because I heard you're the best. So the pressure is on you to come through.

Michael Sisti

The Follow-up

Dear Bradley Fucking Myers,

Master Pro, my ass. The only thing you're the master of is wasting my time. I was pretty clear that I didn't want my swing changed, as I only needed a little tweak. And I allocated a half hour for that simple advice.

You on the other hand, tried to change my grip, my stance, my set up, my weight transfer, and my swing plane. With all those modifications, you pissed away a full hour, and it got me nowhere.

After yesterday's lesson, I played this morning with my regular group and lost $20. I should have you refund me the $20. It was the worst I played in years, certainly worse than before your 'lesson'.

The Retort

Dear Mr. Sisti

Based on your description as a seasoned, skilled golfer, I'm at a loss that you didn't grasp the simple points of the lesson. But I am a trained, certified, Master Professional. I have taught hundreds of students of every age and skill level, some even more dense than you. But they all got something out of the lesson and improved their game.

In your original email you had suggested psychiatric consultation. I'm sorry, but I'm not trained to do that. However, did you do the meditation that I taught you before you played? It could definitely help your state of mind.

I also apologize that I'm not licensed to direct an assisted suicide. However under the circumstances, that would be a definite alternative for you to consider. Given that, I don't think I can be of any further help to you.

BTW. Walmart has golf balls on sale this week. You may want to stock up.

Brad Myers
Certified PGA Master Professional

Going Commando

My friend Frank is a fitness geek. He's a former educator where he was a track coach, plus he played multiple sports when he attended school. Retired for over 20 years, he now stays in peak shape by cycling constantly, and working out three times a week.

About a month ago, we changed our regular Saturday golf game to Friday because there was an outing scheduled for Saturday morning. Our group comprises about 16-20 golfers and we tee off starting at 9 am. Unfortunately for Frank, Friday is his workout day, and being anal, he never alters his schedule.

That morning, Frank got up at 5, ate breakfast, threw his golf clothes in his gym bag, and went to Abs-R-Us at 6. After his one-hour workout, he showered and pulled out his golf shirt and shorts. Unfortunately, he forgot to pack a change of underwear. He thought about washing the pair he worked out in, but they would never dry before his tee-off time. So, making an executive decision, he went 'Commando'.

When Frank showed up at the golf course, he was fidgety and uncomfortable. Trying to dissipate his nervous energy, he told everyone about the wardrobe malfunction and that he was golfing commando. And despite making everyone laugh with his story, Frank was still a little off-center. But then, Frank usually is when he plays golf.

That morning Frank rode in Bob's cart, and I had the good fortune to drive the second cart. We teed off and the round was playing uneventfully, but I noticed that Frank was a little quieter than his usual volatile self. I was sure it was because he thought we all could see through his white golf shorts.

On the eleventh hole, we all had good tee shots that landed in the fairway. Bob's was the shortest, so he played his second shot first. He pulled up alongside his ball within three feet of it, and parked on the right side, even with the cart's seat. As Bob pulled out his three-wood, Frank looked at the proximity of the ball and said, 'Bob, you're really close. Do you want me to move the cart?'

'No, Frank. The cart won't bother me.' As he was saying that, he was already in his backswing, and he made a hellacious swipe at the ball. Unfortunately, Bob's club glanced the ball and it came out at a right angle to the swing. It went straight into the cart at 120 mph, hitting the bottom of the roof, right alongside Frank's skull. It ricocheted off the roof, again missing Frank, hit the steering wheel, and several interior parts of the cart before it came harmlessly to a stop on the grass. Miraculously, it missed Frank's body at least five times, although it grazed his scalp, changing the part in his hair from the left to the right side.

Visibly shaken, Frank tumbled out of the cart, and lay on the ground hyperventilating. At about the same moment he realized that he wasn't dead was when he wished he was wearing underwear.

Made in the USA
Middletown, DE
24 November 2018